HAPPY VALENTINE'S DAY

I COULDN'T DECIDE WHAT TO GET YOU SO...
I GOT YOU A BOOK FULL OF VOUCHERS!

Enjoy!

THIS VOUCHER ENTITLES YOU TO:

ONE SEXY WISH

TERMS & CONDITIONS:
CAN BE REDEEMED AT ANYTIME.
THE COUPON HOLDER CAN HAVE
3 WISHES OF THEIR CHOOSING.
NON-TRANSFERABLE.

0000000000000000

THIS VOUCHER ENTITLES YOU TO A:

MASSAGE

Enjoy!

0000000000000000

TERMS & CONDITIONS:
CAN BE REDEEMED ONLY AT NIGHT TIME.
THE COUPON HOLDER MUST HAVE
SHOWERED WITHIN AN HOUR & MUST LAY
DOWN NAKED. NON-TRANSFERABLE.

THIS VOUCHER ENTITLES YOU TO:

CAR FUN

TERMS & CONDITIONS:
CAN BE REDEEMED AT ANY TIME.
THE COUPON HOLDER OR GF / WIFE
MUST HAVE A CAR. NON-TRANSFERABLE.

THIS VOUCHER ENTITLES YOU TO A:

QUICKIE

Enjoy!

TERMS & CONDITIONS:
CAN BE REDEEMED AT A TIME & PLACE OF
YOUR CHOICE. THE COUPON HOLDER MUST
HAVE SHOWERED WITHIN AN HOUR & MUST
BE STD FREE NON-TRANSFERABLE.

THIS VOUCHER ENTITLES YOU TO A:

MASSAGE

Enjoy!

TERMS & CONDITIONS:
CAN BE REDEEMED ONLY AT NIGHT TIME.
THE COUPON HOLDER MUST HAVE
SHOWERED WITHIN AN HOUR & MUST LAY
DOWN NAKED. NON-TRANSFERABLE.

THIS VOUCHER ENTITLES YOU TO A:

HASSLE FREE NIGHT OUT

WITH THE BOYS

TERMS & CONDITIONS:

CAN BE REDEEMED ONLY AT WEEKENDS.
THE COUPON HOLDER CAN HAVE A HASSLE
FREE NIGHT OUT WITH HIS FRIENDS.
NON-TRANSFERABLE.

0000000000000000

THIS VOUCHER ENTITLES YOU TO A:

CUDDLE SESSION

TERMS & CONDITIONS:
CAN BE REDEEMED AT ANY TIME &
ANYWHERE. NON-TRANSFERABLE.

THIS VOUCHER ENTITLES YOU TO A:

BLOWJOB

Enjoy!

TERMS & CONDITIONS:
CAN BE REDEEMED AT A TIME & PLACE OF YOUR CHOICE. THE COUPON HOLDER MUST HAVE SHOWERED WITHIN AN HOUR & MUST BE STD FREE NON-TRANSFERABLE.

0000000000000000

THIS VOUCHER ENTITLES YOU TO A:

QUICKIE

Enjoy!

TERMS & CONDITIONS:
CAN BE REDEEMED AT A TIME & PLACE OF
YOUR CHOICE. THE COUPON HOLDER MUST
HAVE SHOWERED WITHIN AN HOUR & MUST
BE STD FREE NON-TRANSFERABLE.

0000000000000000

THIS VOUCHER ENTITLES YOU TO A:

LAP DANCE

TERMS & CONDITIONS:
CAN BE REDEEMED ONLY AT NIGHT TIME.
THE COUPON HOLDER MUST ALSO BE NAKED
FOR THE DANCE. NON-TRANSFERABLE.

00000000000000000

THIS VOUCHER ENTITLES YOU TO A:

MAKE OUT SESSION

TERMS & CONDITIONS:
CAN BE REDEEMED ONLY ON THE COUCH.
THE COUPON HOLDER MUST HAVE BRUSHED
THEIR TEETH WITHIN AN HOUR.
NON-TRANSFERABLE.

THIS VOUCHER ENTITLES YOU TO A:

ROLE PLAYING GAME

TERMS & CONDITIONS:
CAN BE REDEEMED ONLY AT NIGHT TIME.
THE COUPON HOLDER HAS THE CHOICE OF
ANY ROLE PLAYNG THAT THEY WISH.
NON-TRANSFERABLE.

0000000000000000

THIS VOUCHER ENTITLES YOU TO:

SHOWER SEX

TERMS & CONDITIONS:
CAN BE REDEEMED AT ANY TIME.
THE COUPON HOLDER MUST HAVE NOT
SHOWERED ON THAT DAY ALREADY.
NON-TRANSFERABLE.

0000000000000000

THIS VOUCHER ENTITLES YOU TO:

ANAL PLAY

TERMS & CONDITIONS:
CAN BE REDEEMED ONLY AT NIGHT TIME.
THE COUPON HOLDER HAS THE
CHOICE OF GIVING OR RECEIVING.
NON-TRANSFERABLE.

THIS VOUCHER ENTITLES YOU TO A:

NEW POSITION

TERMS & CONDITIONS:
CAN BE REDEEMED ONLY AT NIGHT TIME.
THE COUPON HOLDER TRY A NEW SEX
POSITION OF THEIR CHOOSING.
NON-TRANSFERABLE.

0000000000000000

THIS VOUCHER ENTITLES YOU TO:

PHONE SEX

TERMS & CONDITIONS:
CAN BE REDEEMED AT ANY TIME.
THE COUPON HOLDER TXT OR PHONE CALL.
NON-TRANSFERABLE.

THIS VOUCHER ENTITLES YOU TO A:

PLAY WITH

BOOBIES

TERMS & CONDITIONS:
CAN BE REDEEMED AT ANY TIME. THE COUPON HOLDER MUST HAVE ATLEAST 15 MIN BOOB PLAY. NON-TRANSFERABLE.

THIS VOUCHER ENTITLES YOU TO:

3 WISHES

TERMS & CONDITIONS:
CAN BE REDEEMED AT ANY TIME. THE
COUPON HOLDER GET'S A CHOICE OF 3
WISHES. MUST CHOOSE CAREFULLY!
NON-TRANSFERABLE.

0000000000000000

THIS VOUCHER ENTITLES YOU TO A:

STRIP TEASE

TERMS & CONDITIONS:
CAN BE REDEEMED ONLY AT NIGHT TIME.
THE COUPON HOLDER MUST BE NAKED FOR
THE STRIP TEASE. NON-TRANSFERABLE.

0000000000000000

Made in the USA
Las Vegas, NV
13 February 2024

85717865R00026